DON'T LET LIFE GET YOUR *goat*

Published by Sellers Publishing, Inc.

Copyright © 2018 Sellers Publishing, Inc.
All rights reserved.

Sellers Publishing, Inc.
161 John Roberts Road, South Portland, Maine 04106
Visit our Web site: www.sellerspublishing.com • E-mail: rsp@rsvp.com

Mary L. Baldwin, Managing Editor
Charlotte Cromwell, Production Editor
Cover and interior design by Charlotte Cromwell

ISBN 13: 978-1-4162-4644-2

10 9 8 7 6 5 4 3 2 1

Printed in China.

Credits on page 64.

DON'T LET LIFE GET YOUR

goat

KEEP YOUR CHIN UP, KID!

SELLERS
PUBLISHING

FIND YOURSELF A
FRIEND WHO IS A
good listener.

Life has its rhythms.
TAKE TIME TO DANCE.

NEVER TAKE YOURSELF
too seriously.

WHENEVER POSSIBLE,
*choose to take
the high road.*

Be yourself.
EVERYONE ELSE IS
ALREADY TAKEN.

Hold your head high, AND BE CONFIDENT IN ALL THAT YOU DO.

Stand tall

WHEN OTHERS MAKE
YOU FEEL SMALL.

FAILURE IS THE CONDIMENT THAT GIVES *success* ITS FLAVOR.

DO THE THINGS THAT
ring your bell.

AVOID
overthinking
THINGS.

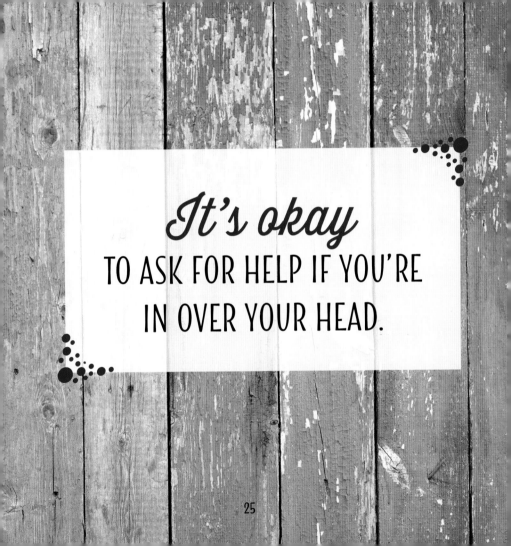

It's okay
TO ASK FOR HELP IF YOU'RE
IN OVER YOUR HEAD.

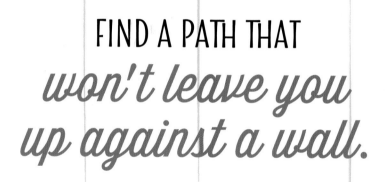

FIND A PATH THAT

won't leave you up against a wall.

Stick your neck out. REMEMBER, GOOD THINGS MIGHT BE RIGHT AROUND THE CORNER.

Celebrate the
little things
THAT MAKE LIFE SWEET.

LIFE IS BETTER

when shared with a friend.

Don't be afraid
TO TAKE A STEP OUT OF YOUR
comfort zone.

DO YOUR BEST
to remain a kid at heart.

THERE IS ALWAYS

strength in numbers.

GO A LITTLE WILD,
it's good for the soul!

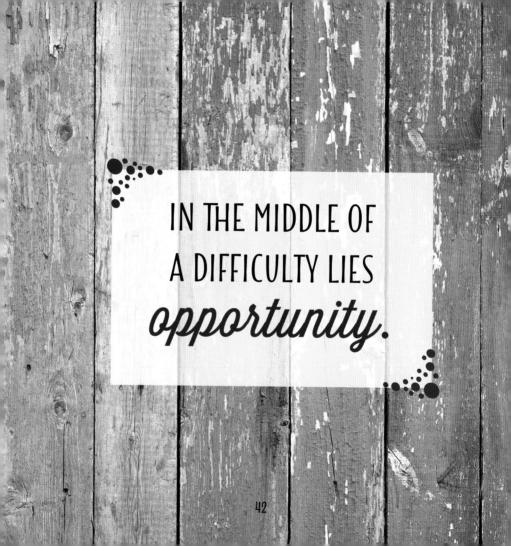

IN THE MIDDLE OF
A DIFFICULTY LIES
opportunity.

"*Family first*"
IS ALWAYS A
GOOD POLICY.

Don't be afraid of change. SOMETIMES THE GRASS REALLY IS GREENER ON THE OTHER SIDE OF THE FENCE.

Head up,
stay strong,
FAKE A SMILE,
MOVE ON.

Surround
yourself
with friends
WHO GET YOU.

IT'S HARD TO
move forward
IF YOU'RE ALWAYS
LOOKING BACK.

Avoid locking horns,

IT WILL BE EASIER TO STAY BALANCED.

A smile is the best WAY TO DISARM AN ADVERSARY.

Those who follow the crowd MAY FIND THEMSELVES AT THE EDGE OF A CLIFF.

BE SOMEONE
that other's look up to.

THE BEST WAY TO AVOID
FEELING DOWN IS TO
*keep your
chin up* .